Linda Evangelista

The True Account Of Her Biography, Untold Story
About Her Health Life, Career, Personal Life, Net
Worth, Achievements, Legacy And Impacts

Evelyn Everlore

Table of Contents

Introduction

In the world of fashion, where dreams are spun from threads of imagination and the runway is a canvas for artistic expression, there exists a constellation of stars. Among them, one shines with a luminosity that refuses to dim—a name synonymous with beauty, transformation, and an enduring legacy. In the pages that follow, we embark on a journey through the life and times of this remarkable icon, a journey that unveils the captivating tale of **Linda Evangelista**. Her story is a tapestry of triumphs, challenges, and the unwavering spirit that has left an indelible mark on the fashion industry and beyond.

Chapter 1

The Early Years

A Glimpse into Linda's Childhood

In the quiet town of St. Catharines, Ontario, amidst the gentle rustling of maple leaves and the cool breeze off Lake Ontario, a star was born on May 10, 1965. Little did the world know that Linda Evangelista, the name that would later grace magazine covers and mesmerize runways, was taking her first breaths in this unassuming Canadian town.

Linda's early years were marked by the simplicity and warmth of her family life. She was born to Italian immigrant parents, Anna and

Tomaso Evangelista, who brought with them the rich heritage of their homeland. Her father, a factory worker, and her mother, a bookkeeper, instilled in Linda the values of hard work, dedication, and the importance of family bonds. It was within the walls of her home that Linda's character began to take shape, and the seeds of her future greatness were sown.

From a tender age, Linda exhibited a vivacious spirit and an undeniable charm. She possessed a magnetic presence that drew people to her, leaving an impression that lingered long after she had left the room. Those who knew her in those early years would often describe her as a vivacious and determined child, unafraid to pursue her dreams, no matter how distant they may have seemed.

As Linda entered her formative years, her curiosity about the world outside of St. Catharines began to grow. She attended Denis Morris Catholic High School, where her academic pursuits were complemented by her growing interest in the arts. It was here that she began to explore her love for fashion and style, often sketching designs and experimenting with different looks.

The small-town girl with big dreams soon found herself at a crossroads. The world outside of St. Catharines beckoned, and Linda knew that to pursue her ambitions, she needed to venture beyond the familiar. Her path to modeling began with a serendipitous encounter that would forever alter the course of her life.

One fateful day, while visiting a local beauty salon with her mother, Linda was spotted by a talent scout. This chance encounter would be the catalyst that propelled her into the world of fashion. The scout, recognizing Linda's unique beauty and presence, saw in her the potential to become a star. It was an offer of opportunity that Linda could not resist.

With the unwavering support of her family, Linda embarked on a journey that would take her far from the comfort of home. Her destination: the bustling city of New York, the epicenter of the fashion universe. At just 19 years old, armed with dreams and determination, Linda Evangelista set forth on a path that would lead her to international acclaim.

The Ascent to the World of Fashion

The streets of New York City are often described as a concrete jungle where dreams are pursued with unrelenting fervor. For Linda Evangelista, these streets became the runway to her destiny. Her arrival in the city that never sleeps marked the beginning of a meteoric rise that would soon see her grace the covers of the world's most prestigious fashion magazines.

In the heart of Manhattan, Linda navigated the competitive world of modeling with a grace and poise that set her apart. She possessed a striking beauty that defied convention—angular features, luminous eyes, and a transformative quality that would make her one of the most sought-after models of her generation.

Linda's ascent in the fashion industry was nothing short of remarkable. She quickly caught the eye of top photographers, designers, and fashion editors. Her versatility was her calling card; she could embody the essence of a sophisticated couture model one moment and effortlessly transition into the role of an edgy, androgynous figure the next.

It was this chameleon-like ability that made Linda a muse to photographers and designers alike. She breathed life into their creative visions, becoming the embodiment of their artistic aspirations. This synergy between Linda and the creative minds of the fashion world would yield iconic images that continue to resonate with audiences today.

As she graced the pages of magazines and walked down prestigious runways, Linda's influence extended far beyond the world of fashion. She was not merely a model; she was a cultural phenomenon, a symbol of a new era where models were celebrated as celebrities in their own right. The '80s and '90s were a time of transformation in the industry, and Linda Evangelista was at the forefront of this evolution.

In the following pages, we delve deeper into Linda's ascent through the fashion ranks, exploring her unforgettable milestones, and the moments that solidified her status as an icon. The early years of her career were marked by boundless ambition and an unwavering commitment to her craft. But as we shall see, Linda's journey had its share of challenges, and the road to superstardom was not without its twists and turns.

Chapter 2

The Supermodel Emerges

The '90s Supermodel Era

The dawn of the 1990s marked a turning point in the world of fashion, and at its epicenter was a seismic shift that would forever alter the industry's landscape—the emergence of the supermodel. It was an era where models transcended the catwalk, gracing the covers of magazines, dominating advertising campaigns, and becoming household names. And leading this formidable pack of supermodels was none other than the incomparable Linda Evangelista.

The '90s heralded a new era of glamour, sophistication, and larger-than-life personalities.

The term "**supermodel**" was coined to describe this elite group of women who were more than just models; they were cultural icons. Alongside Linda, names like Cindy Crawford, Naomi Campbell, Christy Turlington, and Kate Moss became synonymous with beauty, power, and style.

It wasn't merely the fashion industry that these supermodels conquered; it was the hearts and minds of a global audience. With their stunning looks and charismatic presence, they brought fashion into the mainstream, making it accessible to people from all walks of life.

One of the defining moments of this era was the now-iconic Vogue cover from January 1990, featuring Linda Evangelista, Naomi Campbell, Christy Turlington, Cindy Crawford, and Tatjana Patitz. This cover, shot by renowned photographer Peter Lindbergh, would go down in history as a symbol of the supermodel phenomenon. It wasn't just a magazine cover; it was a cultural statement, a declaration that models were the new stars of the moment.

The '90s supermodels weren't just admired for their beauty; they were celebrated for their personalities. Linda Evangelista, with her wit, charm, and undeniable presence, was at the forefront of this revolution. She became known not just for her striking looks but also for her vivacity, her fearlessness in front of the camera, and her ability to transform into myriad personas.

Linda Evangelista: The Chameleon of the Catwalk

One of Linda Evangelista's most remarkable qualities was her ability to morph into different characters with every photo shoot and runway appearance. She was a true chameleon of the catwalk, a model who could seamlessly transition from one look to another, leaving audiences in awe of her versatility.

This transformative quality was what set Linda apart from her contemporaries. She didn't have just one signature look; she had many. Designers and photographers found in her an ideal canvas on which to paint their visions. Whether it was the sultry femme fatale, the androgynous muse, the ethereal goddess, or the edgy rebel, Linda could inhabit these roles effortlessly.

Perhaps one of the most iconic examples of Linda's chameleon-like abilities was her legendary collaboration with photographer Steven Meisel. Together, they created a portfolio of work that remains unparalleled in its influence on fashion and culture. With Meisel behind the lens and Linda in front of it, they pushed boundaries and challenged conventions.

In their work together, Linda transformed into an array of characters, each more captivating than the last. She could be the epitome of '90s minimalism one moment, with sleek, straight hair and understated makeup, and in the next, she would be a '60s bombshell with voluminous curls and bold eyeliner. Her adaptability was a testament to her talent and her willingness to fully immerse herself in the creative process.

Linda Evangelista's influence extended beyond the runway and the pages of magazines. Her style was emulated by countless women worldwide. She set trends, defined looks, and left an indelible mark on the world of beauty. Makeup artists and hairstylists sought to recreate her signature looks, from her striking pixie cut to her sultry smokey eyes.

But Linda's impact wasn't limited to aesthetics; she was also a symbol of empowerment. She embodied the idea that women could be strong, confident, and unapologetically themselves. Her presence on the runway exuded a sense of self-assuredness that resonated with women everywhere. She was proof that you could be both beautiful and powerful, a message that transcended fashion and became a cultural anthem.

In the pages that follow, we will explore the iconic moments and the milestones that defined Linda Evangelista's career as a supermodel. Her ability to transform and transcend the boundaries of fashion would continue to shape the industry, making her a true legend of the catwalk.

Chapter 3

A Career in Full Bloom

Magazine Covers and Iconic Photoshoots

The '90s were an era of unparalleled growth and transformation for Linda Evangelista's career. Her ascent to supermodel status was punctuated by a dazzling array of magazine covers and iconic photoshoots. Each cover represented not just a moment in Linda's career but a cultural touchstone, a testament to her status as one of the most recognizable and influential figures in the world of fashion.

One of the defining moments in Linda's career was her role as the face of Calvin Klein's Eternity fragrance campaign. Shot by Meisel, this campaign captured the essence of love, sensuality, and enduring beauty. Linda, alongside male model Mark Vanderloo, became the embodiment of romanticism. Her ethereal beauty and captivating presence turned what could have been a mere advertisement into an iconic representation of timeless love.

Another milestone in Linda's career was her partnership with photographer Richard Avedon for the Versace Fall 1995 campaign. The images from this campaign remain etched in the annals of fashion history. In one particularly striking photo, Linda, alongside fellow supermodels Christy Turlington and Naomi Campbell, posed as a trio of Amazonian warriors. Clad in bold, empowering designs, they exuded strength and confidence. This campaign was a testament to the transformative power of fashion, and Linda was at its epicenter.

Defining Moments in Linda's Career

Throughout her career, Linda Evangelista encountered moments that not only defined her path but also left an indelible mark on the fashion industry. One such moment was her decision to embrace a radical haircut—a sleek, cropped pixie that became her signature look. In an era where long, flowing locks were the norm, Linda's daring haircut was a statement of individuality. It was a move that only an icon could make, and it propelled her into the realm of timeless style.

Linda's evolution as a model was also characterized by her foray into acting. She made her silver screen debut in Robert Altman's "Prêt-à-Porter" (1994), a satirical take on the fashion industry. Linda played herself in the film, a nod to her status as a fashion luminary. While her acting career didn't rival her modeling success, it was another testament to her versatility and willingness to explore new horizons.

In the midst of her soaring career, Linda Evangelista faced her own share of challenges. She was candid about her struggle with body image and the pressures of the industry. Her openness about these issues added a layer of authenticity to her status as a role model for women everywhere. Linda's willingness to confront these issues head-on humanized her in the eyes of her admirers.

As we delve deeper into Linda's career, we will uncover more of these defining moments, each one a brushstroke on the canvas of her remarkable journey. Her ability to grace magazine covers, transform in front of the camera, and confront the industry's challenges with grace and resilience solidified her status as a true legend of the fashion world.

Chapter 4

A Battle Begins

December 2018: The First Breast Cancer Diagnosis

In the glittering world of fashion, where beauty is celebrated and grace is revered, the unexpected specter of illness can cast a shadow over even the brightest stars. For Linda Evangelista, December of 2018 brought with it a revelation that would test the mettle of even the most resilient soul—a breast cancer diagnosis.

It was a stark reminder that life's script is often filled with unexpected plot twists. As the world continued to admire Linda's timeless beauty and career achievements, she confronted a foe that did not discriminate based on fame or fortune. Breast cancer, a relentless adversary, was now a part of Linda's narrative.

The news of Linda's diagnosis sent shockwaves through the fashion industry and beyond. For those who had admired her from afar, it was a moment of collective concern. Yet, amidst the turmoil of her diagnosis, Linda approached the situation with a spirit that would come to define her journey—a spirit marked by courage and an unwavering resolve.

For Linda, the decision to share her diagnosis with the world was a deeply personal one. She had always been a fiercely private individual, choosing to keep the intricacies of her life shielded from the prying eyes of the public. But in confronting a health challenge of this magnitude, Linda chose to embrace transparency.

The Decision to Undergo Bilateral Mastectomy

Facing a breast cancer diagnosis is a profoundly emotional experience. It is a journey that requires not only physical strength but also an immense amount of courage and self-reflection. For Linda Evangelista, the path forward became clear—an option that would require great sacrifice but offered the promise of a life free from the looming specter of cancer.

In July 2019, Linda made the decision to undergo a bilateral mastectomy—a surgical procedure that would remove both of her breasts. It was a choice that demanded immense bravery, as it meant embracing a transformative change to her physical self. But for Linda, the decision was about securing her future, about taking control of her health and her destiny.

The journey that followed was marked by a series of surgeries, each one a step towards a new beginning. The physical healing was accompanied by emotional and psychological challenges, as Linda grappled with the profound changes to her body. It was a process that demanded resilience and an unyielding spirit, qualities that Linda had demonstrated throughout her career.

As Linda embarked on her path to recovery, she did so with a sense of determination that had defined her career as a supermodel. It was a reminder that even in the face of adversity, Linda Evangelista remained an icon—a symbol of strength and grace.

In the following pages, we will explore the deeply personal and courageous journey that Linda undertook in the wake of her breast cancer diagnosis. Her decision to confront the illness head-on, her choice to share her story with the world, and her unwavering spirit in the face of adversity all serve as a testament to her remarkable character. In a world where beauty is often celebrated but resilience is not always seen, Linda Evangelista's story shines as a beacon of hope and strength.

Chapter 5

Triumph and Setbacks

Life After Surgery: Recovery and Resilience

In the wake of her bilateral mastectomy, Linda Evangelista embarked on a journey of recovery—a path marked by physical healing, emotional resilience, and an unwavering determination to embrace life anew. Her breast cancer diagnosis had been a profound turning point, but it was in the aftermath of surgery that Linda's true strength and character would shine.

The road to recovery was neither swift nor simple. Linda confronted a series of physical and emotional challenges that tested the very essence of her being. She was no stranger to adversity, having faced the demanding rigors of the fashion industry, but this was a different kind of battle, one where the stakes were nothing less than her health and well-being.

In those early days of recovery, Linda drew strength from the unwavering support of her loved ones—her family, friends, and the countless well-wishers from around the world who had been touched by her story. Their encouragement served as a constant reminder that she was not alone in this journey, that her triumph over adversity was a testament to the human spirit's ability to endure and overcome.

As the physical scars of surgery began to heal, Linda found herself confronted with a new reality—one where the absence of breasts posed both a physical and emotional challenge. Yet, true to her resilient nature, Linda embraced this change with a grace that resonated with her admirers. She refused to let her altered appearance define her, recognizing that her beauty and strength transcended physical attributes.

It was during this period of recovery that Linda's decision to share her story with the world took on a new significance. Her openness about her breast cancer diagnosis and the subsequent surgery served as a source of inspiration to countless individuals facing similar challenges. She became a beacon of hope, a living testament to the power of resilience, and a reminder that beauty is not confined to external appearances.

The Unexpected Challenge: Paradoxical Adipose Hyperplasia (PAH)

Just as Linda was on the path to recovery and reclaiming her life, an unexpected challenge emerged—a rare condition known as Paradoxical Adipose Hyperplasia (PAH). This condition, a side effect of a body-contouring procedure known as CoolSculpting, would introduce a new layer of complexity to Linda's journey.

CoolSculpting is a non-invasive procedure designed to eliminate stubborn fat cells. It was meant to be a solution, a way for Linda to regain her confidence and feel comfortable in her own skin once again. However, fate had other plans. PAH, an exceedingly rare side effect of the procedure, led to the opposite result—it caused thickening and swelling of fatty tissue, leaving Linda with a physical challenge she had never anticipated.

The psychological impact of PAH was profound. Linda, who had already faced the emotional hurdles of breast cancer and surgery, now had to confront a new layer of self-doubt and insecurity. The transformation of her body, far from the intended outcome of the procedure, left her feeling disfigured and vulnerable.

In the midst of this unexpected setback, Linda chose to confront PAH with the same resilience that had defined her journey thus far. She shared her struggle with the world, shedding light on the rare condition and the challenges it posed. Her courage in the face of adversity resonated with those who admired her not just for her beauty but for her unyielding spirit.

Linda's decision to publicly address her experience with PAH was not without its challenges. It required a level of vulnerability that few public figures are willing to embrace. Yet, Linda saw it as an opportunity to raise awareness, to let others facing similar obstacles know that they were not alone, and that even in the face of unexpected setbacks, one could find the strength to persevere.

Chapter 6

Legal Battles and Personal Strength

Seeking Justice: Linda's Lawsuit Over Cosmetic Procedure

Linda Evangelista's journey of recovery from breast cancer and the unexpected challenge of Paradoxical Adipose Hyperplasia (PAH) would soon lead her into uncharted territory—a legal battle over the cosmetic procedure that had resulted in her PAH diagnosis.

In the midst of her personal struggles, Linda made the difficult decision to seek justice. She filed a lawsuit against the firm Zeltiq Aesthetics, the company responsible for CoolSculpting ($50 million), the procedure that had led to her PAH. It was a pivotal moment, one that would test not only her personal strength but also her resolve to hold accountable those responsible for her ordeal.

The lawsuit was not merely a legal matter; it was a quest for accountability. Linda's decision to take legal action was driven by a desire to ensure that others would not suffer the same fate. She became an advocate for transparency and safety in the cosmetic industry, using her platform to shed light on the potential risks associated with procedures like CoolSculpting.

The legal battle was not without its challenges. Linda faced a formidable opponent in a complex and protracted lawsuit. The legal proceedings demanded time, energy, and emotional fortitude. Yet, Linda's determination to seek justice remained unshaken. She demonstrated a level of personal strength that transcended the confines of her supermodel status.

Eventually she revealed on her Instagram handle on 5th September 2023, that she is pleased to have settled the lawsuit.

She said,

"I eagerly anticipate the upcoming phase of my life, filled with cherished moments with my loved ones, and I am relieved to leave this issue in the past. I deeply appreciate the support I've received."

The Power of Perseverance

As the legal battle came to an end, Linda Evangelista's resilience came to the forefront once again. She exhibited a rare blend of strength and perseverance, qualities that had defined her journey from the earliest days of her career. The same tenacity that had propelled her to the pinnacle of the fashion industry was now driving her quest for justice.

Linda's decision to share her experiences—both her breast cancer journey and her battle with PAH—served as a source of inspiration to many. Her willingness to confront adversity head-on, to speak openly about her challenges, and to seek accountability demonstrated the power of personal strength. She became a symbol of courage for those facing their own struggles, a reminder that one could navigate even the most daunting obstacles with resilience and determination.

Throughout her career, Linda had been celebrated for her beauty, her versatility, and her ability to transform in front of the camera. But it was her journey beyond the runway, her willingness to confront life's challenges with unwavering strength, that solidified her status as an icon in the truest sense of the word. She showed the world that true beauty transcended physical appearances, that inner strength and resilience were the qualities that truly defined a person's character.

Chapter 7

Return to the Spotlight

A Surprise Comeback: Linda's Return to the Runway

After a period of personal trials, Linda Evangelista made a triumphant return to the world that had celebrated her as one of its most iconic figures—the fashion industry. It was a surprise comeback that defied the odds, a testament to her enduring spirit and resilience.

Linda's return to the runway was met with a sense of anticipation and excitement. The world had watched as she confronted breast cancer, battled Paradoxical Adipose Hyperplasia (PAH), and waged a legal battle over a cosmetic procedure gone wrong. Through it all, Linda had displayed a grace and strength that had resonated with admirers around the globe.

Her announcement that she would appear in a fashion show for Fendi in September captured the imagination of fashion enthusiasts and industry insiders alike. It was a moment that signaled not just a return to modeling but a reclamation of her place in the spotlight.

Linda's presence on the runway was more than just a fashion statement; it was a celebration of resilience. It was a reminder that beauty, grace, and strength are qualities that transcend the passing of time. As she graced the catwalk once again, she carried with her the collective hopes and admiration of those who had followed her remarkable journey.

Gracefully Aging in the Fashion Industry

In an industry where youth is often celebrated, Linda Evangelista's return to the spotlight challenged conventional notions of age and beauty. Her presence on the runway was a powerful statement—a declaration that beauty and style know no age limits.

Linda had always been a chameleon on the catwalk, effortlessly transforming from one look to another. Now, she was redefining what it meant to gracefully age in the fashion world. Her appearance was a testament to the enduring appeal of a true icon—a woman who had not just weathered life's storms but had emerged even more radiant.

As Linda navigated the challenges of the fashion industry, she did so with a sense of wisdom and self-assuredness that can only come with time. Her journey had taught her that beauty was not confined to external appearances but was a reflection of one's inner strength and character. It was a lesson that she shared with the world, reminding us all that true beauty is timeless.

Chapter 8

Linda's Second Breast Cancer Diagnosis

In 2018, Linda Evangelista confronted the formidable adversary of breast cancer for the first time. It was a battle that tested her resolve, demanded immense courage, and ultimately led her down a path to recovery. Yet, four years later, in 2022, she faced a new chapter in her journey—a second breast cancer diagnosis, this time in her pectoral muscle.

The news of her recurrence was met with the same unwavering determination that had defined Linda's journey from the beginning. She faced the diagnosis head-on, expressing her resolute desire to confront the disease with everything she had. Linda recalled telling her surgeon, in no uncertain terms, to "dig a hole in my chest." It was a plea that transcended aesthetics; it was a declaration of her fierce will to fight, to emerge victorious once again.

"I don't want it to look pretty. I want you to excavate. I want to see a hole in my chest when you're done," she had said to her doctors. "Do you understand me? I'm not dying from this."

Her second surgical procedure was a testament to Linda's unyielding spirit. It was a declaration that she would not be defined by her diagnosis, that she would not let cancer dictate the terms of her life. It was a reaffirmation of her commitment to living life to the fullest.

Linda's post-cancer care oncologist described her current prognosis as "good," offering a glimmer of hope amidst the uncertainty. However, the specter of cancer recurrence was not without its weight. Linda revealed that her doctor had given her a "horrible oncotype score," a numerical representation of the risk of cancer recurrence. It was a reminder that even in the face of optimism, the battle was far from over.

Yet, Linda's response to the uncertainty was nothing short of remarkable. She embraced each day as a precious gift, recognizing that life's fragility made every moment more valuable. She declared, "I know I have one foot in the grave, but I'm totally in celebration mode." It was a testament to her indomitable spirit, her refusal to be defined by fear, and her determination to make the most of every moment.

Breast cancer diagnoses were not the only health issues that Linda Evangelista had faced in recent years. Her journey had been marked by adversity, by challenges that tested her strength and resilience. Yet, through it all, Linda remained a symbol of unwavering determination, a reminder that the human spirit's capacity for resilience knows no bounds.

In the chapters that follow, we will delve deeper into Linda Evangelista's extraordinary journey, her resilience in the face of adversity, and her unwavering commitment to living life on her own terms. Her story serves as an inspiration to all, a reminder that even in the darkest moments, one can find the strength to celebrate life's precious moments and face the future with hope and courage.

Chapter 9

Personal Life

Relationships

In 1987, Linda Evangelista entered into matrimony with **Gérald Marie**, who held the position of head at Elite Model Management's Paris office. However, their union ended in divorce in 1993. Her romantic history also included a relationship with actor **Kyle MacLachlan**, a connection that initially sparked on a photoshoot in 1992. Although the couple became engaged in 1995, they eventually separated in 1998. Subsequently, Linda embarked on a relationship with French football player **Fabien Barthez**. During their time together, Linda experienced the joy of pregnancy, yet tragedy struck as she suffered a miscarriage six months into the pregnancy. The couple's relationship encountered several twists and turns, including a breakup in 2000, a brief reconciliation in 2001, and a final separation in 2002.

In a notable turn of events, Linda Evangelista's personal life became a subject of public attention due to a child support case. In October 2006, she welcomed a son named **Augustin James** into the world while deliberately keeping the identity of the child's father a secret, which led to speculations. It was during her pregnancy that she graced the cover of Vogue in August 2006. In June 2011, Linda filed court documents revealing that her son's father was billionaire Frenchman François-Henri Pinault, whom she had dated for a brief four-month period in late 2005 and early 2006. François-Henri Pinault later wed actress Salma Hayek. Linda's quest for child support led her to file for a child support order in Manhattan Family Court on August 1, 2011, seeking a monthly sum of $46,000 from

Pinault. This request, if granted, would have set a record as one of the largest child support orders in the history of family court. The matter proceeded to a highly publicized child support trial commencing on May 3, 2012, with both Pinault and Evangelista providing testimony. Evangelista's legal representative contended that Pinault had never provided support for the child. However, on May 7, 2012, several days into the trial, Evangelista and Pinault reached an out-of-court settlement.

Religion

Regarding her religious beliefs, in a 1997 interview, Linda Evangelista disclosed that she was a devout Roman Catholic and expressed her fondness for the Bible, naming it as her favorite book.

Net Worth

Linda Evangelista is a highly affluent and accomplished Canadian fashion model who has achieved remarkable feats throughout her career. During the 1980s and 1990s, she emerged as one of the most influential and captivating models in the industry. With just a single glance, she possessed the power to captivate hearts. At present, her estimated net worth stands at an impressive **$40 million.**

Chapter 10

Legacy and Impact

The Everlasting Influence of Linda Evangelista

Linda Evangelista's journey in the world of fashion and beyond has left an indelible mark that extends far beyond the runways and glossy pages of magazines. As we explore her legacy and impact, it becomes evident that her influence transcends time, setting her apart as a true icon.

From the moment Linda stepped onto the fashion scene in the mid-1980s, her magnetic presence was undeniable. Her striking features and the chameleon-like ability to transform with every photoshoot set her apart from the crowd. She quickly became known as the model's model, a muse to photographers and designers alike. Her innovative spirit, reflected in her willingness to experiment with her appearance, would not only redefine beauty standards but also pave the way for future generations of models.

Linda's contributions to the fashion industry cannot be overstated. In 1988, she famously took the bold step of chopping her hair, giving rise to her iconic hairstyle. Overnight, it became a sensation, setting trends and inspiring countless imitations. Her ability to dictate style rather than follow it was a testament to her pioneering spirit and refusal to conform to conventional norms.

Her Contribution to Changing Beauty Standards

Linda Evangelista's impact on beauty standards was transformative. In an industry where rigid ideals often reigned supreme, Linda challenged the status. Her versatility and adaptability defied the notion that beauty came in only one form. Through her work, she celebrated diversity, showing that beauty was multifaceted and transcended boundaries.

Linda's advocacy for embracing one's uniqueness was not limited to the camera lens. She empowered individuals to embrace their individuality and authenticity. Her influence extended to the broader conversation on body image, self-confidence, and self-acceptance. She was more than a model; she was a role model.

As the fashion industry evolved, Linda Evangelista's legacy remained unwavering. Her iconic status was cemented when she was named the greatest supermodel of all time in 2008, a title that recognized her enduring influence and the mark she had left on the world of fashion.

Beyond her professional achievements, Linda's personal journey, including her battles with breast cancer and the unexpected challenges of cosmetic procedures, served as a source of inspiration. Her willingness to share her vulnerabilities and her unyielding determination to overcome adversity resonated with individuals facing their own struggles.

Conclusion

In the world of fashion, there are models, and then there are icons. Linda Evangelista, without a doubt, belongs to the latter category. Her life's journey, as we've explored in these pages, is a testament to the power of determination, resilience, and the pursuit of one's dreams.

From her early years, growing up in Canada, to her meteoric rise in the 1980s and 1990s, Linda's story is one of unwavering ambition. She didn't just break boundaries; she shattered them. With her striking looks and the ability to transform herself into a myriad of personas, she became the muse of photographers and designers worldwide. Her contribution to changing beauty standards was not just groundbreaking; it was revolutionary.

Linda Evangelista's legacy extends far beyond her image on magazine covers and runways. She became an advocate for embracing one's uniqueness, inspiring countless individuals to embrace their individuality and authenticity. Her willingness to share her personal struggles, from battling breast cancer to facing the unexpected challenges of cosmetic procedures, resonated with people facing their own trials.

As we reflect on Linda's life and career, we're reminded that true beauty is not confined to external appearances but is a reflection of inner strength and character. Her story serves as an enduring source of inspiration, a reminder that the human spirit's capacity for resilience knows no bounds.

In the ever-evolving world of fashion, where trends come and go, Linda Evangelista's influence remains timeless. She is not just a supermodel; she is a superwoman—a symbol of grace, power, and authenticity. Her legacy continues to shape the industry she once dominated, and her impact on beauty standards endures.

In closing, Linda Evangelista's journey is a testament to the belief that dreams can be realized, boundaries can be shattered, and beauty can be redefined. Her story is not just a biography; it's an ode to the human spirit's ability to triumph over adversity and leave an indelible mark on the world. Linda Evangelista, the supermodel, the icon, the inspiration—her story is one that will continue to inspire generations to come.

Printed in Great Britain
by Amazon

41513663R00036